Quack Some Good Cheer!

Poetry... with Especially You in Mind

Martha Nompone

WestBow Press books may be ordered through booksellers or by contacting:

WestBow Press
A Division of Thomas Nelson & Zondervan
1663 Liberty Drive
Bloomington, IN 47403
www.westbowpress.com
1 (866) 928-1240

ISBN: 978-1-4908-7555-2 (sc)
ISBN: 978-1-4908-7556-9 (e)

Library of Congress Control Number: 2015905181

Print information available on the last page.

WestBow Press rev. date: 04/17/2015

WESTBOW
PRESS
A DIVISION OF THOMAS NELSON
& ZONDERVAN

Dedicated to my Mom

Muddy Mud Puddle

The day has dawned! Up comes the sun!
But your thoughts return to old gloom that's done.
Are you still in that muddy mud puddle?

The air is clear with hope and strength.
New ideas stir! There are good plans to be made!
Are you still in that muddy mud puddle?

Life is happening to your neighbors and friends,
Who chose to get out of the mud they were in.

Excuses upon excuses pour through your mind.
You think that your "good life" is all behind.
"Impossible! I can't! I won't! I'll never!"
Will those words be your close friends forever?

Ready? Choose something else today!
Erase the past! Don't delay!
Small beginnings are fine. It doesn't take much.
Create the first step by hosing off the mud.

"............ the garment of praise for the
spirit of heaviness........."
Isaiah 61:3

My Cat Is So Busy

Peering out a window,
Watching birds go by.
Sitting in the sun's glow,
On the window sill time slips by..........
My cat is so busy.

Lounging on the cozy chair
Eyes hardly open.
At the big fish tank he stares,
Barely even coping..........
My cat is so busy.

Deep in the clothes closet
Hiding behind the shoes.
Finds a stack of blankets
On top he decides to snooze.

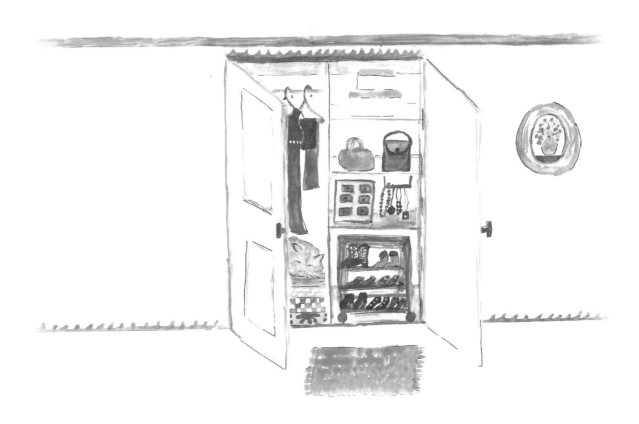

Wouldn't want to bother him
If you're in need of assistance.
His schedule is overloaded to the brim.
You would meet with much resistance,

Because of course.............
My cat is so busy.

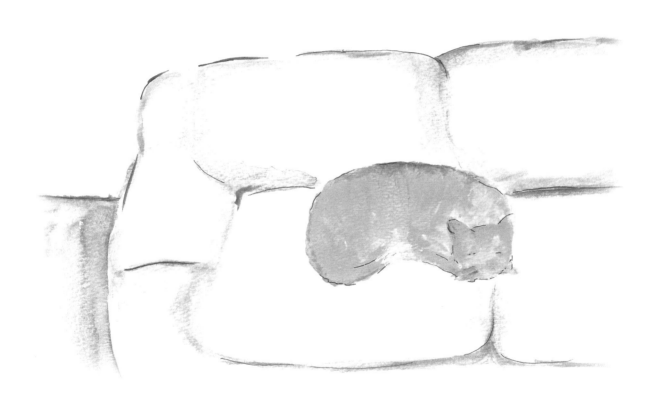

"For so He giveth His beloved sleep."
Psalm 127:2

Orchids Made Her Wild !

Nira was a dressmaker
With her own little shop in the city.
Her day's work was spent sewing,
Making dresses so pretty.

Nira's sewing machine hummed
With perfect perfection.
Buttons and buttonholes made
To connect every connection.

Steady hand stitching
Nira completes exactly right.
A sewn creation is finished.
What a beautiful sight!

Nira lived an orderly life
At home and at work.
BUT THEN! All of a sudden
The orderliness went berserk!

For what did she behold
In the flower shop window that day?
There were wondrous orchid flowers
Whose names she could barely say.

There were various kinds of orchids.
(Nira was informed by the clerk.)
Of course, she bought many different ones.
Most of them didn't even need dirt.

Wow! These orchids are amazing!
Nira soon learned their ways.
Growing and selling lots of orchids
Soon filled up her days.

Oh now there's no time to worry
About what clothes she puts on.
"Comfortable" is now
the theme of Nira's song.

So if you knew Nira
When her life was calm and mild,
You may be surprised now to see
That orchids have made her wild!

"And whatsoever ye do, do it heartily
as unto the Lord.............."
Colossians 3:23

My Mama always had lots to do.
Her work was never done.
But even with piles of dishes and clothes,
She would make time for something fun.

Mama said, "I want to knit you some mittens,
Because I love you so."
"They will be yellow, so sunny and bright,
When out in the snow you go."

I watched Mama knit, using minutes here and there,
And one yellow mitten was finished!

But Mama's spare time, which was needed to knit,
Then became greatly diminished.

My Mama never ever managed to knit
The match to that bright yellow mitten.
But the love that I felt, from the one that she made,
Is the reason this poem was written.

"She seeketh wool, and flax, and worketh
willingly with her hands."
"Her children arise up, and call her blessed..."
Proverbs 31:13 & Proverbs 31:28a

Cottonwood Hearts

Poppy the beautiful poplar tree
Was born in a small backyard.
He stretched and pushed his very best
To work his branches hard.

He knew he had an important message
For all who looked his way.
He knew that God is mighty and great,
But above all, Poppy wanted to say,

"Our great and wonderful holy God
Is full of LOVE for you!
He sent His one and only Son
So all of you could become new."

And if you doubt, I will remind you
Of this gift of love.
Just look what stems down from my branches.
They show the good news from above."

"For clusters of continuous hearts
Weigh on my cottonwood limbs,
Because of the overflowing love
That could only come from Him."

"I'm just one sort of tree," Poppy says,
"in a small backyard, but I stand tall
to tell of the glorious love that comes only
from the Lord and Maker of all."

"For God so loved the world, that He gave His only
begotten Son, that whosoever believeth in Him
should not perish, but have everlasting life."
John 3:16

Inside Outside Puppies

Lulu slowly stretches and stretches
As morning puppies do.
Berkley dances his first little jig
Even though he just woke up too.

Doors of the cozy kennels are open
Then Lulu and Berkley are out!
They bound through the back door and run for the grass
Rejoicing their day is about to start!

Breakfast is served outside by the pool.
Lulu, are you ready? On your mark!
Berkley hopes, if weather permits,
They'll be allowed a run through the park!

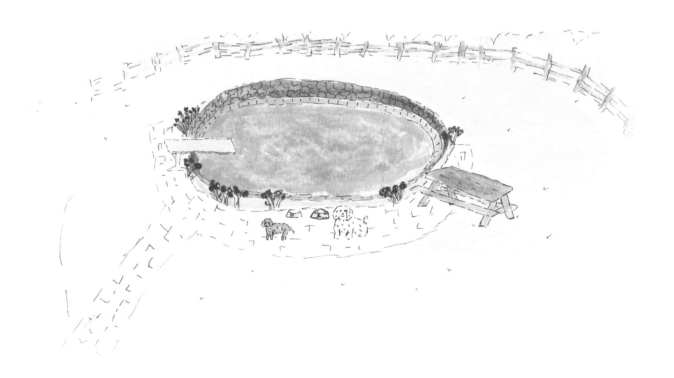

Then the sun disappears and it looks like rain.
Their outside time is done.

The puppies race in, to play on the kitchen floor,
Because inside time is also fun!

When the rain has stopped, then there they go,
Eager again to be out!
Lulu is always first and in the lead.
Berkley is thrilled to follow her about.

So much to experience, so much to see
In a puppy's world without a doubt.
And Lulu and Berkley appreciate their day
Whether they are inside or out.

"..........for I have learned, in whatsoever
state I am, therewith to be content."
Philippians 4:11b

A Skunk Caught In Your Beak?

Beautiful day!
You can see the sunshine!
There are friends in abundance.
Why are your words unkind?

Is there a skunk caught in your beak?

Encouragement is needed
And support for the team!
Celebrate life's treasures!
(No time to be mean.)

Is that skunk still caught in your beak?

New life in the garden. Babies are born.

Awards are earned and your feathers are not torn.

The day's work is challenging, stretching your brain.

Excitement is called for.

Why quack and complain?

Hey, its your choice.
You get to decide
Whether or not
To enjoy the ride.

Quack some good cheer!
Stay away from the rut.
Why keep giving off an odor
From chomping on that skunk?

Words spoken can be healthy,
As vitamins to the soul.
Words can enable
Our minds to grow.

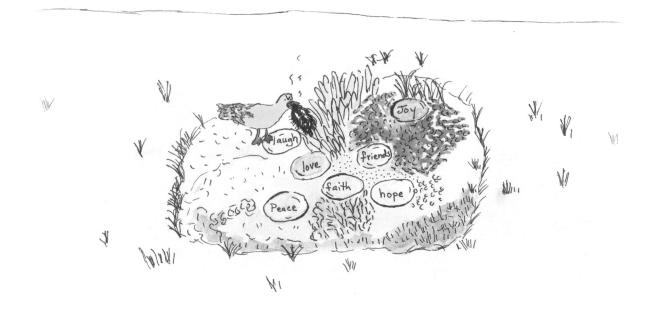

But words mixed with skunk fumes
Can smell and cause pain
To someone whose respect
You may then never gain.

There are burdens others carry
That none of us see.
Adding to their weariness,
We don't want to be.

Words have made a difference
When spoken to you.
Your words will affect
Someone else's life too.

Life has its ups.
Life has its downs.
It's sometimes a jungle
When troubles abound.

You can add to the highs
Or add to the lows.
There is much up to you
As to how your life goes.

So raise your glass to the good!
Appreciate even the small.
Those special little details are gems
If polished at all.

Now as far as your kind words—
Go sing them out by the hunk,
Once you've rinsed out your beak
Letting loose of the skunk.

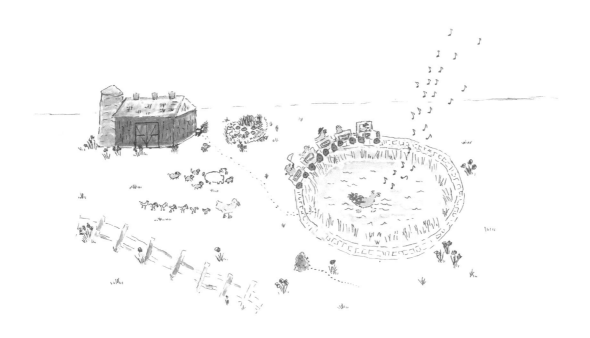

"But now ye also put off all these: anger, wrath,
malice, blasphemy, filthy communication out of
your mouth."
Colossians 3:8

Scriptures taken from the King James Version of the Bible

Printed in the United States
By Bookmasters